Launching Your Life

How to use the business principles
of entrepreneurship to launch a life you love

90-DAY ACTION PLAN WORKBOOK

Erin Moran McCormick

Launching Your Life
How to use the business principles of entrepreneurship to launch a life you love
90 Day Action Plan Workbook

By Erin Moran McCormick

ISBN-13: 978-1542828567
ISBN-10: 1542828562
Published by: Year of Action

CONTACT INFORMATION:

To contact Erin to speak at your organization or event, email:
Erin@YearofAction.com

Check out the programs and workshops at:
www.YearofAction.com
www.LaunchingYour.Life

YOU ARE AMAZING

Most people never get to where you are right now. They don't take the time or make the effort to figure out what they want or how to make it happen. They go through the motions and look back at their life and wonder what might have been.

You are different.

You are here and consciously choosing to create the life you want. You have a unique set of skills and talents to bring to the world. Sometimes these are hard to see or uncover and we give up before we get started. But not you. You are here to make it happen. I believe in you. I am here to help you discover what you need to do to succeed.

Whether you are starting a business, writing a book, taking on a new project at work or feeling a bit lost and overwhelmed right now and not sure where to go next in life - it all starts the same way. You have to believe in the possibility. You have to imagine it. It starts with you and what you are telling yourself. It's your attitude.

Knowledge and hard work will only get you so far. It's your attitude that makes the difference. So, the first part of this journey is about getting in the right mindset. It may require changing some old habits and limiting beliefs. It may mean pushing past the self-doubt. (We are often our own worst critic.)

THE BUSINESS OF LAUNCHING YOUR LIFE

If you ask a seven-year-old what she wants to be when she grows up, she'll give you a list of big dreams:
I want to be an architect, a ballet dancer, a doctor…
I want to go to the moon, to the Olympics, to the Oscars.

At some point we stop dreaming. Reality sets in. We have to pay the bills and find a "real job". Dreams are for kids. Or are they?

We'll teach you how to use the business principles of innovation and entrepreneurship to figure out what you love, what you're great at, what the world needs and what people will pay you for.

That sweet spot is your purpose - your dream. We're here to help you create it.

LAUNCHING YOUR LIFE

PROLOGUE

For the past ten years, I have been working with entrepreneurs, emerging leaders and executives from around the world to help them develop the business skills to succeed in an innovation economy. My clients include GE, Eversource and KPMG and my programs have been featured in FORBES and FOX TV.

I am currently the Director of the Center for Innovation & Entrepreneurship at UMass Boston. I have started three companies, been CIO twice and former Director, Curriculum Innovation & Technology at Babson College - #1 in the world for entrepreneurship education.

As the author of **Year of Action: How to Stop Waiting & Start Living Your BIG, Fabulous Life** and founder of ***Year of Action***, business programs for the innovation economy, I help people take action and get results. I have 50+ product launches under my belt. In other words, I'm pretty good at launching stuff.

The business of launching your life

Most people think they are supposed to magically *just know* what they want to do with their life. Yet – most of us have no clue what to do or where to begin. Having worked with so many people who wanted to take action on their lives, but didn't know what to do or where to begin, I realized something.

You can use the principles for launching a successful product or business as a framework for "launching your life" – throughout the different stages of your career. There are specific steps you need to take to be successful.

You majored in *what?*

Think about it. College majors usually don't naturally align with real-world jobs. (Anthropology of what?) In fact, the first question most people ask when they hear what you majored in is, "What are you going to do with *that*?" We think there's a better answer than shrugging your shoulders and trying to figure it all out on your own.

What if you had a roadmap to show you the steps to take?

Successful entrepreneurs know they need to *start where they are.* They take inventory of what they want, what they have, and what they need, and come up with a plan to get where they want to go. This works for anyone and can be applied to *creating the business of you.*

The next step

You don't have to know *all* the steps, you just have to know the *next* step – and be inspired and supported to take it. This workbook is used in our **Launching Your Life workshops** and will show how you to assess where you are now, figure out where you want to go and teach you the steps to take to get there.

LAUNCHING YOUR LIFE

THE PLAN

This book is divided into 10 steps that follow the framework of how to successfully launch a business or product. It will help give you structure for figuring out how to launch the next version of YOU and help you create a life you love – for any stage of your career.

The 10 steps are:

LAUNCHING YOUR LIFE

1. PASSION

Ahhhh, passion. There is a lot of talk about this. You have probably heard some version of this: "Just follow your passion"; "Do what you love and the money will follow"; or "Build it and they will come." I have to let you in on a little secret: it's not true.

FORGET "FOLLOW YOUR PASSION"

Hear me out. Yes - I wholeheartedly believe that you *can* and *deserve* to LOVE your work, but "Follow your Passion" isn't the whole story. This well-meaning advice actually wreaks havoc on SO many entrepreneurs.

A better piece of advice is, **"Do something you can be passionate about."**

It's not "just" about doing what you love. Just because you love yoga, doesn't mean you should open a yoga studio. You'll spend most of your time on things that have NOTHING to do with yoga: finding customers, paying the rent, getting insurance, finding customers, putting in a billing system, creating a website (did I mention finding customers?) – and actually very little time in *downward dog*. You may even wind up resenting what you once loved. Besides, running a business means you have to love *running a business.*

Instead, the secret is to figure out what you are great at; what value you bring to the table; and what you can contribute to the world that people will pay for. It's about knowing your strengths and leveraging them to do work that you love. It's a variation on the theme.

BE PASSIONATE ABOUT WHAT YOU DO – INSTEAD OF TRYING TO TURN A PASSION INTO WORK.

We want you to be passionate about what you do – and it doesn't mean you have to start a business to do that. *It might.* But for most people, it means bringing an **entrepreneurial mindset** to any career.

Having an entrepreneurial mindset today means knowing how to see opportunities, solve problems in innovative ways and provide value. It means thinking differently about your work. It means consciously creating the career you love. It means turning ideas into action – whether you work at a Fortune 500 company or at your kitchen table.

It means using entrepreneurial skills to create work you love that makes a difference, makes a living, and makes you happy. We can teach you how to use entrepreneurship skills for your life.

LAUNCHING YOUR LIFE

2. PAIN

It starts with pain. A good entrepreneur sees pain as an opportunity. It is an opportunity to solve the pain and provide value. Businesses succeed by taking away pain and providing joy. Less pain. More joy. That's it. We are going to work on how to develop your entrepreneurial mindset and help you turn pain into joy – and create a life you love.

STUCK. OVERWHELMED. OUT OF CONTROL.

I know how it feels. To feel stuck. To feel overwhelmed. To feel out of control. To work hard but feel like you're just spinning your wheels. To doubt yourself. To feel afraid. To feel like everyone else knows what *they* are doing and you're stumbling along on your own.

The good news is it doesn't have to be like this. We are going to turn your pain into action. I'm going to help you develop an entrepreneurial mindset and run a successful business of YOU.

DEVELOP AN ENTREPRENEURIAL MINDSET

Entrepreneurship is a mindset. It is about embracing challenges and having the courage to take action. People think of entrepreneurs as big risk takers – that may be true. It is also true that they are often just taking small steps forward and building momentum.

It starts with opening your eyes – by paying attention, taking a look around and seeing where you are. I call it the "year of action" process:

1. See the moment
2. Believe in the possibility
3. Take a step…and then another one

I have used this process to write a book, start a business, lose weight, live in Paris, create a job I love with a flexible schedule and more. YOU can get whatever you want in life too. But, here's the catch. You have to DO THE WORK.

You have to do things that push you out of your comfort zone. You have to take the *right* actions. Actions that take you from *being busy* to *being productive*. You have to DO something. Take a step. It's not about overnight success, *get rich quick* schemes, or excuses. If you want it, I'm going to teach you how to get it. It's not magic, it's momentum. You can do this. I can help.

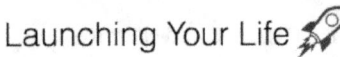

LAUNCHING YOUR LIFE

3. PROCESS

In order to design and develop our product, (you!), we need to set you up for success. These are some tools that will help you figure out what you want and how to get there.

SET YOURSELF UP FOR SUCCESS

This journey starts with getting in the right mindset and getting the tools you need to succeed. It's easy to skip over things that may seem tough or tell yourself that "this" doesn't apply to you. Do me a favor... don't. You're here - so jump in with both feet.

START WITH THESE BASICS:

Write it down

Writing things down – with pen and paper – works. When you write something down, research suggests that our brain *thinks* about us doing it – kind of a visualizing thing – that "tricks" the brain into thinking it is actually doing it. We're processing while we're writing vs. just typing letters on a keyboard.

Writing stimulates cells at the base of the brain, called the Reticular Activating System (RAS). The RAS acts as a filter for what your brain needs to process. When you write it down, the RAS tells the brain to focus on that and your brain will alert you to things to help make that happen.

This workbook has you writing down a lot of things: your goals; all the clutter swimming around in your head; your weekly action items. It's important to *write* them down. Find a pen you love, and do it!

ITZ

In. The. Zone. You have to get *in the zone.* Heads down. Get focused. My kids call it "The Creative Zone", as in, "Mom's in the Creative Zone." Or in kid language, "Don't bug her now."

Multitasking is a myth. Jumping from one task to another is proven to be a bad way to do things. Things actually take longer and aren't done as well. There is a better way to work. You need to work in short focused bursts – like interval training at the gym. Whether it's for 5 minutes, 45 minutes or 90 minutes – concentrated work, works. You are focused on the task at hand and you get it done quickly and efficiently. Then you take a short break and do it again.

PROCESS (continued)

15 minutes

Your first reaction might be, "That would be great to get *in the zone* but that's impossible for me... I'm always interrupted. I have too many things going on at once"... I know. I hear you. Start small. For example, set your timer on your phone for 15 minutes and pick one thing to work on. It could be sending an email, drafting a project outline, making that phone call you've been dreading, or cleaning off your desk. No distractions. No surfing the internet. Just put your head down and go. When the timer goes off, stop. This is great for things that are tough to do, since you know it will be over in a few minutes!

ROA

You've probably heard of ROI - Return on Investment. *ROA* is what I call, Return on Action. Are you taking action on the *right* things? Are you being *busy* or being *productive*? Are you just running around or are you making progress on your goals?

Women are great at making lists and completing tasks - but sometimes we fill up our days keeping busy with little things, that get in the way of actions that could change our lives. It becomes clutter that takes time away from things that we could be doing, that have purpose and help you make progress. What are you doing? Why are you doing it? What is your ROA?

80/20 rule

The 80/20 rule says that 80% of your results are produced by 20% of your effort. Or put another way, if you have 10 customers, two provide the most revenue, but the other eight take up all your time. Or, if you work 10 hours a day, two hours are providing the most results and eight hours are busy work.

The goal is to figure out the 20% that is the most productive and focus on growing that and decreasing the 80%. Cut down or cut out the things that are taking up all of your time and not delivering results.

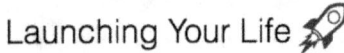

PROCESS (continued)

The Lizard Brain

The "Lizard Brain" is the voice in the back of your head that tells you why you can't do something. *"Don't raise your hand in class." "Don't go on stage." "You can't do that, you don't have the right degree." "You're not that brave." "You wouldn't know where to begin." "You'll fall flat on your face." "You'll look like an idiot." "Everyone will laugh at you." "You will fail." "Don't try anything new." "Stay right where you are." "Do not leave your comfort zone."*

In short, it is fear talking.

It is the oldest part of the brain, the brain stem, responsible for primitive survival instincts. It is called the "Lizard Brain", because it is about all a lizard has for brain function. It is in charge of things like fight or flight, fear and freezing-up. The actual name is the amygdala *(a-mig-da-la).*

You can't get rid of the lizard brain, because it is there to keep you safe. But, it can't distinguish between levels of fear. As far as it is concerned, speaking up in a meeting is the same as being chased by a tiger. If it had its way, it would have you sit in a quiet room by yourself all day and not do anything.

The trick is to embrace the lizard brain - understand that it is there for a reason and find ways to move it to the side. You need to quiet the lizard brain and small action steps work great. Instead of tackling a big goal all at once, you can break it into small action steps and take one step at a time. Small steps aren't as frightening.

For example, when I was thinking about quitting my job and going to Paris, the lizard brain was going crazy - telling me why I couldn't do it. *"You don't speak French." "You don't have any money." "You don't know anyone in Paris." "You don't know what you're going to do." "You can't do it."* All valid reasons.

But, you have a choice. You can let the lizard brain dictate how you are going to live your life, or you can take action. You can take one small step in that direction.

I bought a French dictionary. I figured out how to get a passport. I picked up freelance work to make some extra money. I signed up for a French class… Before I knew it, I had an apartment overlooking the Eiffel Tower. One step at a time. Each step quieted the lizard brain. Eventually, the voice that is stopping you, disappears.

You can start to be aware of the lizard brain and start thinking about what it is that is actually stopping you. Think about ONE STEP you could take to push past the lizard brain roadblock…and take it. Repeat.

PROCESS (continued)

Take control

Email, surfing the web and social media. You can lose HOURS with these. We need to get control of them, instead of having them control us. You don't have to stop what you are doing every time you get an email. Turn off the bell. Get out ahead of it. People have thousands of emails in their inbox and use it as a *To Do List*. This is stressful and makes you feel like you're always behind and never getting things done. Plus, you will waste so much time searching for emails.

There are MANY options for systems to help you get control of your email. Try a few until you find one that works for you. You can just start by checking your email for 5 minutes every hour. Get in the zone while you do it and take action as you check each one - either **delete it, delegate it, defer it** (to an action list to work on) or **do it** (if it's under two minutes).

Law of diminishing returns

In short, this means that the longer you work on something, the less effective you are. Don't drain the battery. It's better if you take a break - whether that be 5 minutes, an hour at lunch, or getting a good night's sleep. You need this. It's a fact. You are more productive when you are alert and refreshed. This goes against the grain for many of us *work horses* – who keep plowing along. I know. I do this too. But I force myself to take breaks. Get a fresh perspective, recharge the battery and clear your head.

Sprints

In software development, they use *sprints* to accomplish short-term, fast-paced goals. You work on one specific piece of a project for a short period of time (a week or two) and then present it to the larger team. This focused work allows you to quickly achieve your goals. It prevents you from going too far down a path before you get feedback and make adjustments. Plus, the frequent check-ins keep you accountable.

Sprints are about setting clear, small goals with a short deadline and going "all in" to meet this goal. It's a structured way to stay focused on what's important. We will use a variation on the sprint theme to achieve your goals.

PROCESS (continued)

B-SASi (Be Sassy)

Many people cringe at the thought of making goals. Too often we "set them and forget them." You may think about failed New Year's resolutions and don't believe in creating goals. It can feel like a waste of time. They seem unattainable and uninspiring. But, it's not about coming up with some vague, long-term goal where you start strong for a week - and then give up. There's a better way.

It's about getting excited about a big, bold dream and making it come alive. You turn the dream into small, short-term, specific goals that you can actually achieve. You then determine what actions will provide the most value to reach those smaller goals and schedule those into your week. You start seeing progress right away with actions that deliver results. I call it B-SASi.

B - **BIG,** bold dream
S - **SMALL**, specific goals
A - **ACTIONS** that get results
Si - **SCHEDULE IT** to make it happen

Go BIG. Start SMALL. ACTIONS for results. SCHEDULE IT. We'll be using the B-SASi method to make your big dreams happen.

One of the biggest complaints I hear from people is that it's hard to focus. You have so many responsibilities and distractions, that it's easy to get knocked off track. You feel like you're all over the place bouncing from one thing to another and not making progress.

With the B-SASi method, you are going to set a big goal and break it into smaller chunks and determine the actions that will provide the most value to achieve those goals. Then you will schedule those actions into your week to make them happen. If it's not in your calendar, it's not real. It doesn't happen. So we have a planner for you to write in your action steps on a specific day - and make it happen.

HOW DO YOU START?

Now that you have some strategies for success, how do you know where to start or what to do? How do you know your goals and action steps? The following pages have questions and exercises to help you get clear on what you want. (Even if you think you know what you want, these are a nice refresher.)

Let's start by talking about dinner.

PROCESS (continued)

GO TO THE STORE OR GO TO THE FRIDGE?

Imagine you're having friends over for dinner. You decide you want to make chicken parmesan. You make a list and go to the store to buy chicken, pasta, tomato sauce, cheese and more.

But what if people are arriving in an hour and you don't have time to go to the store? You open the fridge and see that you have eggs, green peppers and cheese. Guess what? We're having quiche for dinner.

Saras D. Sarasvathy, professor at the University of Virginia Darden School of Business, describes these as two types of entrepreneurs: Causal and Effectual.

Causal is "going to the store." You have a goal and then search for ways to reach this goal. You create an idea, write a plan, finance the plan and execute the plan.

Effectual is "going to the fridge." You start with what you have and look for possible goals. You use what you have. You ask yourself: Who do I know?, What do I know?, What can I achieve?

START WITH WHAT YOU HAVE

As you are thinking about launching the life you love, we'll start with the Effectual, "going to the fridge" method - using what you have. Let's start where you are. Take an inventory of you.

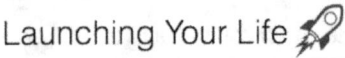

LAUNCHING YOUR LIFE

4. PRODUCT

You are the product. It's your job to make the "business of you" successful, however *you* define success. We will use the "go to the fridge" model and start with what we have. We'll start by figuring out what the "product of you" has to offer and how we launch it, to solve problems and add value.

This section will help you work on how to design and develop yourself to deliver a product that solves a painful problem and adds immense value.

3 SIMPLE QUESTIONS

Sometimes the simple things are the hardest to do. There are three questions you need to ask yourself:

1. Where are you now?
2. Where do you want to go?
3. What do you need to do to get there?

Simple, right? Well - not really. We set up a lot of roadblocks for ourselves. We let fear and doubt and procrastination and busy work and excuses get in the way. These exercises can help you answer these three questions and get clear, get a plan and get going.

Q1. WHERE ARE YOU NOW?

Give us a quick snapshot of where things are now for you in your career and your life. Don't hold back, just tell it like it is. What are you doing now?

____

____

____

____

____

____

____

____

____

____

PRODUCT (continued)

WHICH STAGE ARE YOU AT?

IN TRANSITION

I am thinking about trying something new. I have a lot of ideas and not sure what to do or what makes the most sense.

WHERE PEOPLE GET STUCK:
I bounce around from one idea to another. I worry about whether I can really do it. Lots of fears and doubts creep in. I'm not sure how to get started and I'm not making any progress.

EARLY STAGE

I am at the early stage of something new. There aren't enough hours in the day. I don't know where to focus.

WHERE PEOPLE GET STUCK:
I am overloaded trying to do everything. I'm not quite sure what to do or where to focus and feel a little out of control. I'm working so hard but feel like I'm not getting anywhere.

THE NEXT LEVEL

I have a business (or career) that I want to take to the next level. I have some traction, but I'm not sure where I go from here.

WHERE PEOPLE GET STUCK:
I spend so much time keeping my head above water. I don't know how to put systems in place to get out of the spin. I want to make more income and more of an impact.

I am at the ______________ stage.

OTHER NOTES ABOUT WHERE YOU ARE NOW:

____

____

____

____

____

____

PRODUCT (continued)

Q2. WHERE DO YOU WANT TO GO?

Whatever stage you are at (Think, Start or Grow) you need to think about where you are now, where you want to go and what you need to do to get there.

This is where many people get stuck. We don't know where we want to go or how to get there - so we stay where we are. We don't give ourselves the luxury of taking a step back and thinking about what we are doing or where we want to go. We keep ourselves busy doing what we're doing, and don't take time to ask ourselves why or what we want.

Take some time and go through these next few pages and get clear on where you want to go - and why. There are also some sheets later in the workbook during the *Project Plan* stage to track where your time is going. Keep track for a week. You will be amazed to see where you are spending time.

WHAT'S NEXT?

A great question to ask yourself is, "What's next?" What do I have to do *next?* You don't have to know *all* the steps, you just have to know the *next* one. One step at a time.

We think we are supposed to intuitively *know* what we want to do and where we want to go - with it all mapped out for us. The secret is, there is no map. The map only starts to appear when you take action. It starts to become clear when you take a step. Then you look around, see where you are, make any adjustments and take another step. The map gets clearer with each step.

ACT. ASSESS. ADJUST. *REPEAT.*

You start with some kind of destination in mind. Then you need to take a step, any step, in that direction.

It's like taking a trip. You pick a destination. You get in the car. You get going. You may run into detours. You may have to change your plans. You may decide you want to go somewhere else. You may get a flat tire. It's about continuing to assess where you are and what you need to do to get where you want to go.

You need to continually act, assess and adjust. You keep your focus on what you want - the result - and find new routes and bridges and off-ramps to get you where you want to go.

This is also a good time to think about whether starting and running a business is right for you. You may want to work at a start-up, or be a freelancer or be an intrapreneur (an innovator inside a company), or an entrepreneur. Let's look at your dreams, your skills, what you love (and what you don't love) and see how to put the pieces together into a career you love. Let's take a look at the type of things that you are doing now and where you want to go.

PRODUCT (continued)

TAKE A *JOY* INVENTORY

Sometimes the answer to what we want is right in front of us. You may be close to doing work you love and it just needs some modifications. Take a look at where you are now in your work. (If you are in transition, think about a recent job you have had.) Start by thinking about what you love doing.

I HAD A GREAT DAY AT WORK, I...

When you had a great day at work, what were you doing? What made it great? What makes you feel energized and confident? What makes you feel good? *Meeting new people? Creating great spreadsheets? Coming up with new ideas?* Write down what a great day looks like and the things you are doing.

Imagine that you could get rid of some things that you don't like doing now and add in new things that you love. What would that look like? What do you want to:

DO *MORE* OF AT WORK?

DO *LESS* OF AT WORK?

START DOING?

STOP DOING?

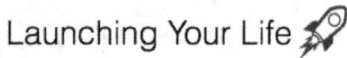

PRODUCT (continued)

PEOPLE ALWAYS ASK ME TO HELP THEM WITH...

What comes easily to you? *Hosting a big event? Redesigning a friend's website? Getting things done quickly?* Just because "it's easy" for you, doesn't mean that it doesn't have value. What do people always ask you to help them with? What kinds of things come "naturally or easily" to you?

ASK OTHERS WHAT *THEY* THINK YOU'RE GOOD AT...

You're easy to work with. You turn chaos into order. You can handle so many things at once and stay calm. You have fabulous style. You inspire people. You run a great meeting... Sometimes others see what we can't. What kinds of compliments do people give you? Ask 3 people what THEY think you're good at - when they have seen you at your happiest, most engaged and productive. (Return the favor and tell them what you think they are good at too.)

PRODUCT (continued)

DO A *SKILLS* INVENTORY

From the "go to the fridge" perspective, let's see what you are naturally great at now. Look over these last few pages and summarize your learnings here. When you are at your happiest and most productive, what are you doing? What skills are you using? What do people always ask you to help them with? What do others say you're good at? If you could spend all day doing something, what would you do?

____

____

____

____

____

____

____

Here are some ideas to get you thinking. Which best describe you? Or write in your own options.

- ☐ Working with my hands
- ☐ Building and fixing things
- ☐ Studying math or science
- ☐ Solving problems and puzzles
- ☐ Working with computers
- ☐ Singing, acting, dancing, or playing music
- ☐ Being creative (writing, art, etc.)
- ☐ Speaking or performing in front of others
- ☐ Helping people solve problems
- ☐ Helping people feel better
- ☐ Teaching people how to do things
- ☐ Leading projects and people
- ☐ Selling things or ideas
- ☐ Being in charge of people
- ☐ Taking technology classes
- ☐ Working with numbers
- ☐ Being organized
- ☐ Following a set plan
- ☐ Learning about history and geography
- ☐ Caring for family and home
- ☐ Working quietly on your own
- ☐ ____________________
- ☐ ____________________
- ☐ ____________________
- ☐ ____________________
- ☐ ____________________
- ☐ ____________________

GOOGLE SKILLS

Do some searches for the skills you have identified and see what kinds of jobs need these skills. How could you apply these skills into your work now? (This will be a work in progress.)

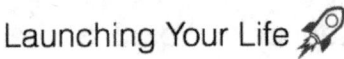

PRODUCT (continued)

DREAM BIG

Something magic happens when you start to imagine what is possible. You don't have to have all the answers or the roadmap now, you just have to believe in the possibility.

Imagine it's a year from now and you just finished your amazing *Year of Action*. You were unstoppable. Money was no object. You couldn't fail. You had the support and guidance you needed to make it happen. What did you accomplish? What incredible things happened?

Imagine it. Write it down. It can be anything. *I signed a $200,000 deal. I worked from home on my own schedule. I doubled my income. I worked 3 days a week. I started a business. I wrote a book. I hit 10,000 followers. I took a month off. I created a dream job and my boss approved it. My team launched the company's biggest project.*

You don't have to know *how* you are going to do it – you just have to want it and be willing to work for it. No filters. What happened in your amazing *Year of Action*?

I HAD THE MOST AMAZING *YEAR OF ACTION*, I...

PRODUCT (continued)

GET REAL

You CAN have an amazing *Year of Action*. You CAN start achieving incredible results. It starts by dreaming big and imagining the possibility; which you just did in the *Amazing Year of Action* exercise! Now, let's go from imagining it, to turning dreams into reality.

These next few pages will help you to get specific about what you want, what you love and your skill set.

MY LIST OF BIG DREAMS

Building off of *Your Amazing Year of Action* exercise, write down what you would really love to do this year. What's the big dream? You don't have to know how you are going to do it now. You just have to want it and be willing to work to make it happen. What do you want? Write your dreams here and why it is important to you? Why do you want it?

BIG DREAM	WHY IT IS IMPORTANT/WHY I WANT IT

We're going to come back to these after a little break and you've had a chance to let them settle in.

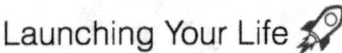

PRODUCT (continued)

THE PERFECT JOB

Usually, the perfect job doesn't exist. You have to create it. It starts by imagining what it looks like. Write down the things you would love. Get specific. Think of things like how much money you want to make, what the office is like and what types of skills you want to use. Dream big. Imagine it here.

Salary ______________________ Hours/Schedule ______________________

What industry? Why? ______________________

Work on your own? Manage others? Types of people there?

In a big company? Small company? Out of your home? ______________________

Commute time? Amount of travel? ______________________

Skills you want to use (that you're good at, are needed, you feel confident and happy while doing them)

Who do you think has a dream job? Why? ______________________

What types of jobs do you find yourself looking at/seem interesting? Why?______________________

Do a search on top/cool/best companies to work for. Write down the ones that seem interesting. Why? What do you like about them? ______________________

PRODUCT (continued)

TOP 10

These are the Top 10 most important things I want in a job:

1. ______________________________
2. ______________________________
3. ______________________________
4. ______________________________
5. ______________________________
6. ______________________________
7. ______________________________
8. ______________________________
9. ______________________________
10. ______________________________

TOP 3: NON-NEGOTIABLE – THESE ARE MY "MUST HAVEs"

These are the most important things to me. They are non-negotiable. For example, it has to meet a certain minimum salary level, or you won't take a job that requires significant travel each week.

1. ______________________________
2. ______________________________
3. ______________________________

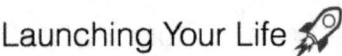

PRODUCT (continued)

PUTTING THE PIECES TOGETHER

THINGS I LOVE	THINGS I'M GOOD AT	THINGS I GET PAID FOR

I HAVE A GREAT DAY WHEN I	PEOPLE ASK FOR MY HELP WITH	OTHERS SAY I AM GOOD AT

THINGS I WANT TO DO MORE OF	THIINGS I WANT TO DO LESS OF	TOP THINGS I WANT IN A JOB

This is the start of your roadmap. Do you see any connections? You can start connecting the pieces of what you love, what skills others value and what you want to do more of and less of. Some pieces may jump out at you and others will take longer to discover what to do with them.

PRODUCT (continued)

MY BIG, BOLD DREAM

Take a look over these last few pages and look at the dreams you have written down. It's time to narrow them down. We want you to focus on one big dream and two smaller dreams that you want to work on over the next 90 days. Make sure that it's something you really, truly want, because we are going to jump in and start to take action to make it happen. Don't worry that you don't know *how* to do it, or if it seems impossible. You just have to choose something that matters to you and you are willing to work towards.

MY BIG, BOLD DREAM IS:

1. ______________________________

CHOOSE 2 SMALLER DREAMS:

2. ______________________________

3. ______________________________

Are you serious?

When you read through these dreams, are you excited about them?

If not, keep going until you come up with three things that you would love. It's not what someone else wants for you, but what YOU want. You don't have to know HOW you are going to make these happen. You just have to know that you want them to happen and you are committed to doing the work.

I PROMISE

This is your life. It happens right now. Make a promise to yourself. Commit to it. If not now, when?

You can do this. We can help, but it is going to be up to you to do the work and make it happen. Once we get started, things are going to start to happen, so we want you to be sure these are things you want.

I, ______________________________, declare that I am *Launching My Life* in the next 90 days and I am committed to making it happen.

CONGRATULATIONS

You did it! You have committed to Launching Your Life. Buckle up - here we go.

PRODUCT (continued)

Q3. WHAT DO I NEED TO DO TO GET THERE?

Now that you have your 3 dreams, what do you need to do? We are going to use the B-SASi model: **BIG** dreams. **SMALL** steps. **ACTIONS** for results. **SCHEDULE IT.** We'll explain it on the next few pages.

WHAT'S STOPPING YOU?

What has been stopping you from making progress on your big dream?
It is usually one of these things:

You don't believe you can do it.
You don't know what to do.
You don't know how to get started.
You don't have time to do it.
You are working on it, but it's not working.
You know what to do, but you're stuck and can't get started.

What's stopping you?

Those things are history. You are creating a new reality – starting right now.

LAUNCHING YOUR LIFE

5. PROBLEM

One of the main reasons that entrepreneurs fail is they forget about the pain.

They start with an *idea,* instead of starting with a problem. They fall *in love* with their idea. They spend all their time and money and focus on developing their idea. All day. All night. Creating. Developing. Building. Tweaking. Tweaking some more. And some more. They do all of this *before* they ever talk to a customer.

By the time they emerge from the garage with their cool new gadget, and finally look around, they realize that no one needs what they built. They forgot about the problem they are trying to solve - or if there even *is* a problem to solve.

The VALUE is in solving the problem, not in the idea. It *may* be a clever idea - but if it doesn't solve a pressing problem, no one will buy it. They should have fallen in love with fixing the problem.

It's NOT about you.
It's ALL about you.

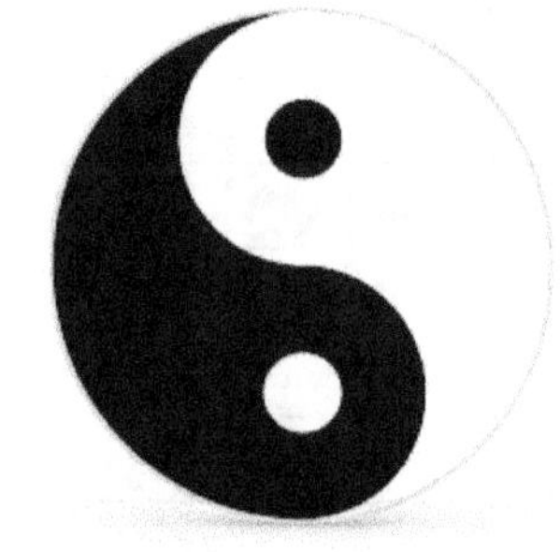

You need to remember that it's not about creating something you like - it's about creating something that solves a problem. It's about providing value to someone in pain.

It's like Yin and Yang. In Chinese philosophy, Yin and Yang means having two opposing concepts exist in harmony.

In our case, it is not about what *you* want, but what the customer wants. At the same time, it is *all* about what you want. What are your unique skills and talents that can provide value? What is the work that you want to do?

As you are thinking about your career or resume or interview - it is a two-way street. It is not about what YOU want. It is about what the company wants. What do they need? How can you provide value to them? At the same time, it is about what you want, what you need, what will make you happy to produce your best work. One of these alone is not enough. They need to co-exist.

What problem can you solve for someone? How can you add value?

LAUNCHING YOUR LIFE

6. PITCH

Have you heard about the "elevator pitch?" Imagine your ideal client steps into the elevator with you, what do you say? How do you get them to say, "Wow!" and give you their card to contact them?

You only have a few seconds. Entrepreneurs practice making their pitch to investors. Investors typically want to know what problem they solve, what are the costs and how much money they have made.

For your personal pitch, it's about the same. What value do you provide (what problem can you solve) and can you make the company money or save them money? It takes practice to create "the perfect pitch." Also, it's best to have different pitches at the ready for different audiences.

UVP - Unique Value Proposition

What is special about you? How do you stand out from the competition? How do you combine your skills and experience to provide unique value?

One of the most common questions you are asked is, "What do you do?"

You can either give a generic answer, "I'm a copywriter." Or you can **describe** what you do in terms of the **value** you provide or the **results** you get: "I help companies get 50,000 new followers quickly."
"I create marketing campaigns that help companies increase their revenue by at least $30,000 a month."
"I help companies develop raving fans like Apple has."

How can you describe what you do in terms of the value you provide? What are the results you get? What do you deliver?

____

____

____

____

____

____

____

____

Practice coming up with a 30-second pitch that describes your UVP. What is your pitch?

LAUNCHING YOUR LIFE

7. PEOPLE

Who do I know?

From the "go to the fridge" example, we learned to start with a few simple questions. The first is: Who do you know? **YOUR NETWORK IS ONE OF YOUR MOST VALUABLE ASSETS**. You need to nurture and grow your network. Start early. Start today.

It doesn't mean you have to go to countless networking events where you don't know anyone and hand out your business cards. You *can* do that – but if you're like me, I cringe at the thought of that. Instead, start by looking at who you know. Here are some tips to get you started.

Build up your "favor bank." Start by helping.

Start doing favors for people. Start solving small problems. Don't be that person who just shows up when they need something. You want to be building up your *favor bank* long before you ever need to draw on any favors.

If you ARE working now, think of how you can help your boss or others at work. Listen for words like, "headaches, challenging, issues, frustrating, so busy, pressure, long hours." These words should set off an alarm for you. These are problems that need solving.

How could you use YOUR special skills to help solve them? Could you collect the data in a spreadsheet for them? Could you make a few sales calls? Could you create a web page? Write some blog posts? Set-up an online invitation? Make a video?

Build a reputation as someone who solves problems and gets stuff done. Be someone who helps others. You will get back much more than you give. Just start helping.

If you ARE NOT working now, you can build this into your conversations. When you meet with friends, ask them about their work. What are they working on? Are they stuck or struggling with anything? You've got some time and could help, at no charge. You may want to get into that field and want to see what it's like. You may do it for a recommendation/ review that you could use, if you do a good job.

[**Quick note:** This is not to say you have to work for free. You deserve to be paid for your work. In the beginning though, you may need to get some experience under your belt and take on some work to prove yourself and get some happy clients. Once you have some solid experience, it's time to start charging.]

PRODUCT (continued)

Dream companies

What are some of the companies/industries you are interested in? You wrote down some interesting companies in an earlier exercise. Do you know anyone working there? Or a friend of a friend? (See LinkedIn below for tips about how to do this.) Connect with them and see if you can set up an informational interview. Remember to ask if there is anything that you can do to help them. Help others.

Use social media

Social media can take control of you or you can take control of it. There are tools to help you manage this and use your time effectively. If you don't know where to begin, ask someone to help you. There's no excuse not to be using social media. Take it one step at a time and get going.

Be careful what you post

Companies will often ask you to show them your Facebook or Instagram pages during the hiring process. What will it show? Is *this* what you want them to see? Think about how you are being perceived. Make sure that what you want to come through is coming through. You are marketing yourself with these tools. It is your reputation. Be smart.

Develop your LinkedIn Profile.

Social media is changing all the time. As of this writing, LinkedIn is still the place you want to be for work connections. The first thing someone does after meeting you or seeing your resume, is check your LinkedIn profile.

Develop your LinkedIn Profile.

Here are some basics you need to do:

a. Have a professional looking headshot.
b. Use keywords in your title - *Recent Grad seeking entry-level programming position*
c. Grow your connections to at least 500. (Don't just send the generic request to connect. Write a sentence or two about how you know that person or why you would like to connect. This is much more compelling than the generic message, and people will be more likely to accept your invitation if you take the time to write something personal.)
d. Let people know you are looking for work. Update your status field - that goes out to your network - *Sarah is looking for a finance position. Do you know anyone who is hiring?*
e. Link to your portfolio or samples of your work

There are many tutorials on how to best use LinkedIn to find people and to be found. (You can make "creating a strong presence on LinkedIn" one of your 90 day goals.) Make it easy for people to find you and to see what you can do for them.

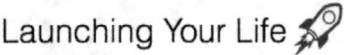

PRODUCT (continued)

My network

You may not think you have a big network, but you'd be surprised. You never know when a friend, old boss, someone next to you while you're getting your hair cut, knows someone who could help you.

Start by jotting down names of people you know.
Start getting in the mindset of growing your network. Let's start brainstorming to get you started. Who could you reach out to? People in organizations/groups you belong to? Family friends? What industries are they in? Who do THEY know? What about their significant others or relatives?

You can start here in the space below to get you thinking of who is in your network and then switch to a spreadsheet or even a free CRM (Customer Relationship Management) tool that sales people use to keep track of it. A couple examples are **Zoho** or **Highrise**.

Name **Industry** **Contact Info** **Notes**

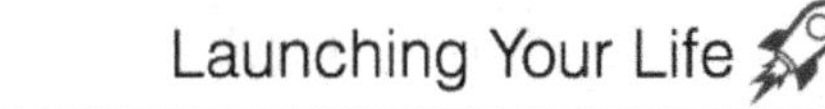

PRODUCT (continued)

Make it easy for people to help you

Put yourself in their shoes. People are busy. They don't have a lot of time. They don't know what you're looking for or your skillset. Make it easy for them.

Be Specific.
Don't give vague statements. "I'm looking for a job - I'll do anything." That doesn't help them. You need to give them something specific to grab on to or remember, so when they hear about openings they'll think of you. Use things from your *Perfect Job* exercise to help you. If you know the types of companies you are interested in, ask your connections if they know anyone in any of those firms.

Don't ask to "pick their brain."
This is a personal pet peeve of mine. You have to earn time with someone. (Remember the "build your favor bank" section.) Instead of asking someone to meet you for coffee or lunch, can you start with a quick question? Can you do it in email or on the phone? Be clear on what you want.

Do your homework.
Research the person and the company. Understand what they do. Look at their social media sites and get a sense of their industry, who their competitors are, what their business model is. Check out their press mentions and latest twitter posts.

Also, think of them like a customer. Can you see where they need help? How can you help them?

What to say/How to say it

The best advice, is keep it short and to the point. What do you want? How can they help? Here are some email basics:

Clear subject line: *Quick question, Connection, Idea*

Short personal greeting: *Short, sincere personal touch – explain who you are and how you are connected.*

Start 1 sentence summary: *State your purpose right up front. What's your question, what do you want them to do?* Don't write a book. Your email should only be a few sentences max. Make it easy for them to scan it quickly and respond. If you are asking for a meeting, give a specific time with a few options. *Do you have time Thursday or Friday morning this week for a quick chat?*

Proof it: Read it over before you send it to see if it is clear. Did you include the attachment you mentioned? Check for any typos. Put your best self forward and make a good first impression.

PRODUCT (continued)

Reach out to people

Once you have your professional profile, and you know what you want to ask someone, how do you connect with people? Let's say you find a great company, and want to connect with the VP of Marketing. Most websites do not disclose the contact information for individuals. Instead, they send you to a generic contact form.

Instead of having to guess if their email is j.bigwig or j_bigwig or jane_bigwig@greatcompany.com, there are tools to help you. Here are a couple:

Hunter (hunter.io)
This free tool searches emails for you and gives you its best guess, and tells you how confident it is that this is the correct email. Plus, if you use Google Chrome as your browser, while using LinkedIn, it gives you a search button to click, to get their email right then. Try it. You'll love this.

Voila Norbert (voilanorbert.com)
Same idea as Hunter and easy to use.

What do I know?

Another part of the "go to the fridge" example is assessing "what do you know." How can you easily show someone what you know and the value that it has?

Show don't tell.
Do you have a way to show your results vs. just talking about them? For example, you could find companies that you are interested in and do your research. Imagine if you worked for them, what could you do? Is there a way to show them?

Check out their website. What can you learn? What kinds of jobs are they advertising? Can you figure out where they are stuck or what they need? How is their social media presence? Their editorial copy? Their marketing efforts? Could you do anything to help? Write up a sample blog post to send them? Make a quick instructional video explaining how to use their product? Could you send them some information of interest?

MVP

Think of how you can *show* your value. Entrepreneurs call this their MVP - Minimum Viable Product. They create a quick prototype to show their idea. Instead of building out an app, they create a draft or mock-up of it in powerpoint to show their customers how it will work. What is something you can create to show your value?

LAUNCHING YOUR LIFE

8. PROFIT

Money. This is one area that *trips up* a lot of entrepreneurs. They get so involved with the product, that they forget about the finances. Or they don't know what their costs are or their profit margins. Or they don't have enough cash flow to stay in business.

Do you know what your monthly costs are? How much do you need to make? Can you afford to take a lower paying job that you love, and still pay the bills? If you are thinking of going into business on your own, have you looked at the numbers? Do you know what it is going to cost? In our *Launching Your Life* workshops, we go through the financials in detail, but for our purposes here, let's get you the basics.

Monthly Expenses

Rent/Mortgage	
Internet/Cable	
Utilities	
Car payment	
Phone	
Insurance	
Memberships	
Commuter pass/expenses	
Gas	
Loans	
Food	
Entertainment/Leisure	
TOTAL MONTHLY EXPENSES:	

Monthly Revenue

Monthly Net Salary (After deductions – your take home pay)	
Additional sources of revenue:	
TOTAL MONTHLY REVENUE:	

Total monthly revenue: ____________

minus total monthly expenses: - ____________

Net Income: ____________

As you are considering salary and job offers and negotiations, remember that there are other options to ask for in addition to the salary. You can negotiate for other things that are important to you such as: additional vacation days, flex time, a bonus, an earlier review, matching 401K, education reimbursement, a better title, an office, parking, health club, childcare, computer, phone…

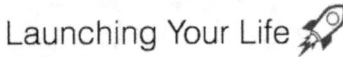

LAUNCHING YOUR LIFE

9. PROJECT PLAN: B-SASi Method

1. BIG DREAM: I want to make $100,000 this year

You don't have to know *all* the steps to reach your big dream, you just have to know the *next* step. We will use the B-SASi method: ***Big** dreams.* ***Small** goals.* ***Actions** for results.* ***Schedule it.*** We break the big dream into small goals. Then we create action steps to achieve these goals. These worksheets can help you figure out the roadblocks and action steps to get past them. Then we'll add the action steps into the weekly planner, later in this workbook.

2. SMALL GOALS

BREAK THE DREAM INTO THESE SMALL GOALS

- I need to make $8,500 a month
- I need to know what my most profitable activities/products are
- I need to know where I add the most value
- I need a plan to increase my revenue

3. ACTION STEPS TO REACH THE GOALS

ACTION STEPS THAT WILL BRING RESULTS	WHAT'S STOPPING ME?	WHAT ONE STEP COULD I TAKE?
• Review yearly sales	I don't know where my files are	Spend 15 minutes a day pulling
• Review top customers	to figure out my top customers	together my invoices
• Create 5 revenue ideas		Start a spreadsheet of customers
• List 10 ideal clients		and invoice totals and sort by $
• Contact 2 potential clients		
	I don't know who are ideal clients	Google other companies in the same
		industry as my top clients
	I don't know how to reach	Update my LinkedIn profile
	potential clients	Find people I know who can connect
		me to people at some of my ideal
		companies

↑ **(You schedule these ACTION STEPS into specific days on your calendar – later in the workbook)**

PROJECT PLAN (continued)

1. BIG DREAM: ____________________

You don't have to know *all* the steps to reach your big dream, you just have to know the *next* step. We will use the B-SASi method: ***Big** dreams. **Small** goals. **Actions** for results. **Schedule it.*** Let's break this big dream into small, achievable goals. Then look at what action steps are needed to achieve these goals. You can use this page as your main worksheet and add the action steps into the weekly planner.

2. SMALL GOALS

BREAK THE DREAM INTO THESE SMALL GOALS

3. ACTION STEPS TO REACH THE GOALS

ACTION STEPS THAT WILL BRING RESULTS	WHAT'S STOPPING ME?	WHAT ONE STEP COULD I TAKE?

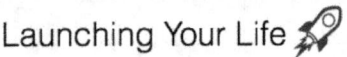

PROJECT PLAN (continued)

1. BIG DREAM: ______________________________

You don't have to know *all* the steps to reach your big dream, you just have to know the *next* step. We will use the B-SASi method: ***Big** dreams.* ***Small** goals.* ***Actions** for results.* ***Schedule it.*** Let's break this big dream into small, achievable goals. Then look at what action steps are needed to achieve these goals. You can use this page as your main worksheet and add the action steps into your weekly planner.

2. SMALL GOALS

BREAK THE DREAM INTO THESE SMALL GOALS

3. ACTION STEPS TO REACH THE GOALS

ACTION STEPS THAT WILL BRING RESULTS	WHAT'S STOPPING ME?	WHAT ONE STEP COULD I TAKE?

PROJECT PLAN (continued)

1. BIG DREAM: ______________________________

You don't have to know *all* the steps to reach your big dream, you just have to know the *next* step. We will use the B-SASi method: ***Big** dreams. **Small** goals. **Actions** for results. **Schedule it.*** Let's break this big dream into small, achievable goals. Then look at what action steps are needed to achieve these goals. You can use this page as your main worksheet and add the action steps into your weekly planner.

2. SMALL GOALS

BREAK THE DREAM INTO THESE SMALL GOALS

3. ACTION STEPS TO REACH THE GOALS

ACTION STEPS THAT WILL BRING RESULTS	WHAT'S STOPPING ME?	WHAT ONE STEP COULD I TAKE?

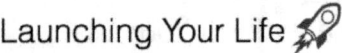

PROJECT PLAN (continued)

4. SCHEDULE IT

If it's not in your calendar, it doesn't happen. It's not real. You need to make it real and schedule it. So the final step of the B-SASi model is to schedule it into your week. Below is an example for how to fill out this Planner at the **beginning of each week.**

It takes all the things "swimming around in your head" and gets them into "buckets" or columns. You can see everything you have to do for the week - *at a glance.* It helps you prioritize what to do *and* find a time when you can do it. Your actions for the week are driven by your goals.

The top half of each page is for a **category** you create: *dream, work, personal, etc.* Each column is a category. The bottom half is a **calendar**. You take each *Action Step* from a column and put it on a specific day to do.

Step 1:

You personalize each of the columns with the important things going on in your life this week: *Dreams (Make $100,000), Work, Birthday Dinner, etc.*

Step 2:

Write the top things to do THIS WEEK under each category. You write the *Small Goals* and the *Action Steps* to meet those goals.

For example, under **MAKE $100,000** you have *Review yearly sales* as a Goal and *Find Invoices* as an Action Step.

In the second column, under **WORK** is *Give Presentation* as a Goal and *Finish Powerpoint* as an Action Step.

Step 3:

At the bottom of the page, write in your appointments and meetings.

Step 4:

Now, take each Action Step that you wrote up top, and find a spot for each one on a specific day. For example, you will *Finish Powerpoint* on Monday and *Find Invoices* on Tuesday.

WEEK OF ________

"YOU CAN'T DO IT, UNLESS YOU CAN IMAGINE IT."
- George Lucas

Write down all the things *swimming around in your head* to do. Put each one under a category (dreams, work, etc.) or create a new category.

Break the dreams into small pieces. Then write what *Action Steps* you can take **this week** to make progress on those pieces.

Put the items from each category on a specific day.

MY BIG, BOLD DREAM IS:	DREAM 2 IS:	DREAM 3 IS:	NOTES ABOUT DREAMS
❶ MAKE $100,000	WORK	BIRTHDAY DINNER	
THE SMALL GOALS:	THE SMALL GOALS:	THE SMALL GOALS:	
Review yearly sales	Give Presentation	Bob's 30th B-Day	
❷ Review top customers	Sales Mtg		
Create 5 revenue ideas			
ACTION STEPS:	ACTION STEPS:	ACTION STEPS:	
Find invoices	Finish Powerpoint	Confirm #s	
Start customer spreadsheet	Create Budget	Order Cake	

❹ MONDAY	TUESDAY	WEDNESDAY	THURSDAY
Finish Powerpoint	Find invoices	Create Budget	Start customer spreadsheet
Confirm #s			Order Cake
❸ APPOINTMENTS/MTGS:	APPOINTMENTS/MTGS:	APPOINTMENTS/MTGS:	APPOINTMENTS/MTGS:
10 am Staff Mtg		12 Lunch w/ Steve	

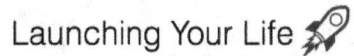

You can use the DREAM ACTION SHEETS in this workbook to help you to figure out your Action Steps. They help you to identify what is stopping you and what one step you can take to push past the roadblocks. Then you put these Action Steps into your Weekly Planner.

There is also a place at the top right page of the Planner for you to identify the three most important things to accomplish this week. What HAS to happen this week? This helps you start to prioritize your goals and action steps.

THE 3 MOST IMPORTANT THINGS TO ACCOMPLISH THIS WEEK:

1. Finish the Powerpoint
2. Work on the Budget
3. Review Yearly Sales

WORK	PERSONAL		
TOP PRIORITY:	TOP PRIORITY:	TOP PRIORITY:	TOP PRIORITY:

There are a limited number of spaces on the Planner on purpose.

You only have so many hours in the day.

It helps you to get clear on what is important, where you need to spend your time and where you need to find help, delegate, push something back or drop it from being a priority.

This helps you to step back and look at your week and decide where you are going to spend your time and what is most important.

Ideally, you can find a time on Sunday or Monday to sit down each week and fill out the Planner so you know what to focus on (and what *not* to focus on) each week.

"YOU CAN'T DO IT, UNLESS YOU CAN

IMAGINE IT."

- George Lucas

WEEK OF ____________________

Write down all the things *swimming around in your head* to do. Put each one under a category (dreams, work, etc.) or create a new category.

Break the dreams into small pieces. Then write what *Action Steps* you can take **this week** to make progress on those pieces.

Put the items from each category on a specific day.

MY BIG, BOLD DREAM IS:	DREAM 2 IS:	DREAM 3 IS:	NOTES ABOUT DREAMS
THE SMALL GOALS:	THE SMALL GOALS:	THE SMALL GOALS:	
ACTION STEPS:	ACTION STEPS:	ACTION STEPS:	

MONDAY ______	TUESDAY ______	WEDNESDAY ______	THURSDAY ______
APPOINTMENTS/MTGS:	APPOINTMENTS/MTGS:	APPOINTMENTS/MTGS:	APPOINTMENTS/MTGS:

THE 3 MOST IMPORTANT THINGS TO ACCOMPLISH THIS WEEK:

1. ______________________________

2. ______________________________

3. ______________________________

PROJECT PLAN (continued)

WORK	PERSONAL		
TOP PRIORITY:	TOP PRIORITY:	TOP PRIORITY:	TOP PRIORITY:
OTHER:	OTHER:	OTHER:	OTHER:

FRIDAY ______	SATURDAY ______	SUNDAY ______	NOTES
APPOINTMENTS/MTGS:	APPOINTMENTS/MTGS:	APPOINTMENTS/MTGS:	

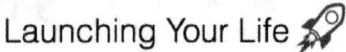

"I DON'T FOCUS ON WHAT I'M UP AGAINST.
I FOCUS ON MY GOALS
AND I TRY TO IGNORE THE REST."

- Venus Williams

WEEK OF ____________________

Focus on your goals and don't worry about the rest. What do you want to focus on this week? Write it all down under a category.

Then choose what is important to do **this week** and write each item on a specific day.

MY BIG, BOLD DREAM IS:	DREAM 2 IS:	DREAM 3 IS:	NOTES ABOUT DREAMS
THE SMALL GOALS:	THE SMALL GOALS:	THE SMALL GOALS:	
ACTION STEPS:	ACTION STEPS:	ACTION STEPS:	

MONDAY ______	TUESDAY ______	WEDNESDAY ______	THURSDAY ______
APPOINTMENTS/MTGS:	APPOINTMENTS/MTGS:	APPOINTMENTS/MTGS:	APPOINTMENTS/MTGS:

THE 3 MOST IMPORTANT THINGS TO ACCOMPLISH THIS WEEK:

PROJECT PLAN (continued)

1. ______________________________

2. ______________________________

3. ______________________________

WORK	PERSONAL		
TOP PRIORITY:	TOP PRIORITY:	TOP PRIORITY:	TOP PRIORITY:
OTHER:	OTHER:	OTHER:	OTHER:

FRIDAY ______	SATURDAY ______	SUNDAY ______	NOTES
APPOINTMENTS/MTGS:	APPOINTMENTS/MTGS:	APPOINTMENTS/MTGS:	

"WE ARE WHAT WE REPEATEDLY DO.
EXCELLENCE,
THEREFORE, IS NOT AN ACT BUT A HABIT."

- Aristotle

WEEK OF ____________________

Let's get in the habit of excellence. Write down all the things that you are thinking about doing. Put each one under a category (dreams, work, fun, etc.)

Then choose what is important to do **this week** and write each item on a specific day.

MY BIG, BOLD DREAM IS:	DREAM 2 IS:	DREAM 3 IS:	NOTES ABOUT DREAMS
THE SMALL GOALS:	THE SMALL GOALS:	THE SMALL GOALS:	
ACTION STEPS:	ACTION STEPS:	ACTION STEPS:	

MONDAY ______	TUESDAY ______	WEDNESDAY ______	THURSDAY ______
APPOINTMENTS/MTGS:	APPOINTMENTS/MTGS:	APPOINTMENTS/MTGS:	APPOINTMENTS/MTGS:

THE 3 MOST IMPORTANT THINGS TO ACCOMPLISH THIS WEEK: :

PROJECT PLAN (continued)

1. ______________________________

2. ______________________________

3. ______________________________

WORK	PERSONAL		
TOP PRIORITY:	TOP PRIORITY:	TOP PRIORITY:	TOP PRIORITY:
OTHER:	OTHER:	OTHER:	OTHER:

FRIDAY ______	SATURDAY ______	SUNDAY ______	NOTES
APPOINTMENTS/MTGS:	APPOINTMENTS/MTGS:	APPOINTMENTS/MTGS:	

"IT'S KIND OF FUN TO DO THE IMPOSSIBLE"

- Walt Disney

WEEK OF ____________________

You're doing it! Keep going and have some fun. What do you want to do? You can choose to do ANYTHING. Write it down.

Then choose what is important to do **this week** and write each item on a specific day.

MY BIG, BOLD DREAM IS:	DREAM 2 IS:	DREAM 3 IS:	NOTES ABOUT DREAMS
THE SMALL GOALS:	THE SMALL GOALS:	THE SMALL GOALS:	
ACTION STEPS:	ACTION STEPS:	ACTION STEPS:	

MONDAY ______	TUESDAY ______	WEDNESDAY ______	THURSDAY ______
APPOINTMENTS/MTGS:	APPOINTMENTS/MTGS:	APPOINTMENTS/MTGS:	APPOINTMENTS/MTGS:

THE 3 MOST IMPORTANT THINGS TO ACCOMPLISH THIS WEEK: :

PROJECT PLAN (continued)

1. ______________________________

2. ______________________________

3. ______________________________

WORK	PERSONAL		
TOP PRIORITY:	TOP PRIORITY:	TOP PRIORITY:	TOP PRIORITY:
OTHER:	OTHER:	OTHER:	OTHER:

FRIDAY _______	SATURDAY _______	SUNDAY _______	NOTES
APPOINTMENTS/MTGS:	APPOINTMENTS/MTGS:	APPOINTMENTS/MTGS:	

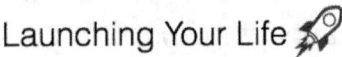

"IT IS NEVER TOO LATE

TO BE

WHAT YOU MIGHT HAVE BEEN."

- George Eliot

WEEK OF ____________________

The best time to start something is TODAY. You can do this. You are making it happen. Keep going. Write down all the things you want to do.

Then put the important things to do on a specific day.

MY BIG, BOLD DREAM IS:	DREAM 2 IS:	DREAM 3 IS:	NOTES ABOUT DREAMS
THE SMALL GOALS:	THE SMALL GOALS:	THE SMALL GOALS:	
ACTION STEPS:	ACTION STEPS:	ACTION STEPS:	

MONDAY ______	TUESDAY ______	WEDNESDAY ______	THURSDAY ______
APPOINTMENTS/MTGS:	APPOINTMENTS/MTGS:	APPOINTMENTS/MTGS:	APPOINTMENTS/MTGS:

THE 3 MOST IMPORTANT THINGS TO ACCOMPLISH THIS WEEK: :

PROJECT PLAN (continued)

1. ____________________

2. ____________________

3. ____________________

WORK	PERSONAL		
TOP PRIORITY:	TOP PRIORITY:	TOP PRIORITY:	TOP PRIORITY:
OTHER:	OTHER:	OTHER:	OTHER:

FRIDAY ______	SATURDAY ______	SUNDAY ______	NOTES
APPOINTMENTS/MTGS:	APPOINTMENTS/MTGS:	APPOINTMENTS/MTGS:	

AERODYNAMICALLY, THE BUMBLEBEE SHOULDN'T BE ABLE

TO FLY

BUT THE BUMBLEBEE DOESN'T KNOW THAT
SO IT GOES ON FLYING ANYWAY."

- Mary Kay Ash

WEEK OF ____________________

Keep believing. Push past the doubts and do it anyway. One step at a time. Write it down. You know the drill.

Then choose what is important to do **this week** and write each item on a specific day.

MY BIG, BOLD DREAM IS:	DREAM 2 IS:	DREAM 3 IS:	NOTES ABOUT DREAMS
THE SMALL GOALS:	THE SMALL GOALS:	THE SMALL GOALS:	
ACTION STEPS:	ACTION STEPS:	ACTION STEPS:	

MONDAY ______	TUESDAY ______	WEDNESDAY ______	THURSDAY ______
APPOINTMENTS/MTGS:	APPOINTMENTS/MTGS:	APPOINTMENTS/MTGS:	APPOINTMENTS/MTGS:

THE 3 MOST IMPORTANT THINGS TO ACCOMPLISH THIS WEEK: :

PROJECT PLAN (continued)

1. ____________________

2. ____________________

3. ____________________

WORK	PERSONAL		
TOP PRIORITY:	TOP PRIORITY:	TOP PRIORITY:	TOP PRIORITY:
OTHER:	OTHER:	OTHER:	OTHER:

FRIDAY ______	SATURDAY ______	SUNDAY ______	NOTES
APPOINTMENTS/MTGS:	APPOINTMENTS/MTGS:	APPOINTMENTS/MTGS:	

"I KNOW FOR SURE THAT WHAT WE

DWELL ON

IS WHO WE BECOME."

- Oprah Winfrey

WEEK OF ____________________

The power of positive thinking. Focus on what you want. See it happening. Write it down. Give it a day. Make it happen.

MY BIG, BOLD DREAM IS:	DREAM 2 IS:	DREAM 3 IS:	NOTES ABOUT DREAMS
THE SMALL GOALS:	THE SMALL GOALS:	THE SMALL GOALS:	
ACTION STEPS:	ACTION STEPS:	ACTION STEPS:	

MONDAY ______	TUESDAY ______	WEDNESDAY ______	THURSDAY ______
APPOINTMENTS/MTGS:	APPOINTMENTS/MTGS:	APPOINTMENTS/MTGS:	APPOINTMENTS/MTGS:

THE 3 MOST IMPORTANT THINGS TO ACCOMPLISH THIS WEEK: :

PROJECT PLAN (continued)

1. ______________________________

2. ______________________________

3. ______________________________

WORK	PERSONAL		
TOP PRIORITY:	TOP PRIORITY:	TOP PRIORITY:	TOP PRIORITY:
OTHER:	OTHER:	OTHER:	OTHER:

FRIDAY ______	SATURDAY ______	SUNDAY ______	NOTES
APPOINTMENTS/MTGS:	APPOINTMENTS/MTGS:	APPOINTMENTS/MTGS:	

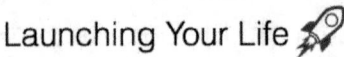

"HOW WONDERFUL IT IS THAT

NOBODY NEED WAIT

A SINGLE MOMENT BEFORE BEGINNING TO IMPROVE THE WORLD."

- Anne Frank

WEEK OF ____________________

It only takes a moment to decide to live the life you want to live. Write down what that looks like.

Then choose what to do **this week** and write each item on a specific day.

MY BIG, BOLD DREAM IS:	DREAM 2 IS:	DREAM 3 IS:	NOTES ABOUT DREAMS
THE SMALL GOALS:	THE SMALL GOALS:	THE SMALL GOALS:	
ACTION STEPS:	ACTION STEPS:	ACTION STEPS:	

MONDAY ______	TUESDAY ______	WEDNESDAY ______	THURSDAY ______
APPOINTMENTS/MTGS:	APPOINTMENTS/MTGS:	APPOINTMENTS/MTGS:	APPOINTMENTS/MTGS:

THE 3 MOST IMPORTANT THINGS TO ACCOMPLISH THIS WEEK: :

PROJECT PLAN (continued)

1. ____

2. ____

3. ____

WORK	PERSONAL		
TOP PRIORITY:	TOP PRIORITY:	TOP PRIORITY:	TOP PRIORITY:
OTHER:	OTHER:	OTHER:	OTHER:

FRIDAY ______	SATURDAY ______	SUNDAY ______	NOTES
APPOINTMENTS/MTGS:	APPOINTMENTS/MTGS:	APPOINTMENTS/MTGS:	

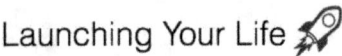

"NEVER CONFUSE MOTION WITH ACTION"

- Benjamin Franklin

WEEK OF ___________________

It's not about being busy and running around. It's about choosing what to do. *ROA. Return on Action.* Take the right actions that move you towards your goals.

Take a look at where your time is going and what you are doing. Trade in *being busy* for *being productive.*

MY BIG, BOLD DREAM IS:	DREAM 2 IS:	DREAM 3 IS:	NOTES ABOUT DREAMS
THE SMALL GOALS:	THE SMALL GOALS:	THE SMALL GOALS:	
ACTION STEPS:	ACTION STEPS:	ACTION STEPS:	

MONDAY ______	TUESDAY ______	WEDNESDAY ______	THURSDAY ______
APPOINTMENTS/MTGS:	APPOINTMENTS/MTGS:	APPOINTMENTS/MTGS:	APPOINTMENTS/MTGS:

THE 3 MOST IMPORTANT THINGS TO ACCOMPLISH THIS WEEK: :

PROJECT PLAN (continued)

1. ____________________

2. ____________________

3. ____________________

WORK	PERSONAL		
TOP PRIORITY:	TOP PRIORITY:	TOP PRIORITY:	TOP PRIORITY:
OTHER:	OTHER:	OTHER:	OTHER:

FRIDAY ______	SATURDAY ______	SUNDAY ______	NOTES
APPOINTMENTS/MTGS:	APPOINTMENTS/MTGS:	APPOINTMENTS/MTGS:	

WEEK OF ____________________

Do away with fear. Write down all the amazing things you are going to do. Make up your mind and do them.

WHEN ONE'S MIND IS MADE UP, THIS

DIMINISHES FEAR;

KNOWING WHAT MUST BE DONE DOES AWAY WITH FEAR"

- Rosa Parks

MY BIG, BOLD DREAM IS:	DREAM 2 IS:	DREAM 3 IS:	NOTES ABOUT DREAMS
THE SMALL GOALS:	THE SMALL GOALS:	THE SMALL GOALS:	
ACTION STEPS:	ACTION STEPS:	ACTION STEPS:	

MONDAY ______	TUESDAY ______	WEDNESDAY ______	THURSDAY ______
APPOINTMENTS/MTGS:	APPOINTMENTS/MTGS:	APPOINTMENTS/MTGS:	APPOINTMENTS/MTGS:

THE 3 MOST IMPORTANT THINGS TO ACCOMPLISH THIS WEEK: :

1. ______________________________

2. ______________________________

3. ______________________________

PROJECT PLAN (continued)

WORK	PERSONAL		
TOP PRIORITY:	TOP PRIORITY:	TOP PRIORITY:	TOP PRIORITY:
OTHER:	OTHER:	OTHER:	OTHER:

FRIDAY _______	SATURDAY _______	SUNDAY _______	NOTES
APPOINTMENTS/MTGS:	APPOINTMENTS/MTGS:	APPOINTMENTS/MTGS:	

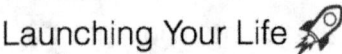

The world is full of people who have dreams of playing at **Carnegie Hall, of running a marathon and of owning their own business.** The difference between the people who make it across the finish line and everyone else is one simple thing:

AN ACTION PLAN"

- John Tesh

WEEK OF

____

It's not magic, it's momentum. It's about believing in the possibility and taking a step. It's about creating a plan of action.

MY BIG, BOLD DREAM IS:	DREAM 2 IS:	DREAM 3 IS:	NOTES ABOUT DREAMS
THE SMALL GOALS:	THE SMALL GOALS:	THE SMALL GOALS:	
ACTION STEPS:	ACTION STEPS:	ACTION STEPS:	

MONDAY ______	TUESDAY ______	WEDNESDAY ______	THURSDAY ______
APPOINTMENTS/MTGS:	APPOINTMENTS/MTGS:	APPOINTMENTS/MTGS:	APPOINTMENTS/MTGS:

THE 3 MOST IMPORTANT THINGS TO ACCOMPLISH THIS WEEK: :

PROJECT PLAN (continued)

1. ____________________

2. ____________________

3. ____________________

WORK	PERSONAL		
TOP PRIORITY:	TOP PRIORITY:	TOP PRIORITY:	TOP PRIORITY:
OTHER:	OTHER:	OTHER:	OTHER:

FRIDAY ______	SATURDAY ______	SUNDAY ______	NOTES
APPOINTMENTS/MTGS:	APPOINTMENTS/MTGS:	APPOINTMENTS/MTGS:	

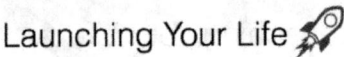

"WHAT WOULD LIFE BE IF WE HAD NO

COURAGE

TO ATTEMPT ANYTHING"

- *Vincent Van Gogh*

WEEK OF ____________________

You are unstoppable. You are taking action. You can do this. Keep taking steps and pushing past the fears and doubts. You decide how you want to live your life.

Choose how you want to spend your time. Dream big. Take a step. *Year of Action!*

MY BIG, BOLD DREAM IS:	DREAM 2 IS:	DREAM 3 IS:	NOTES ABOUT DREAMS
THE SMALL GOALS:	THE SMALL GOALS:	THE SMALL GOALS:	
ACTION STEPS:	ACTION STEPS:	ACTION STEPS:	

MONDAY _______	TUESDAY _______	WEDNESDAY _______	THURSDAY _______
APPOINTMENTS/MTGS:	APPOINTMENTS/MTGS:	APPOINTMENTS/MTGS:	APPOINTMENTS/MTGS:

THE 3 MOST IMPORTANT THINGS TO ACCOMPLISH THIS WEEK: :

PROJECT PLAN (continued)

1. ______________________________

2. ______________________________

3. ______________________________

WORK	PERSONAL		
TOP PRIORITY:	TOP PRIORITY:	TOP PRIORITY:	TOP PRIORITY:
OTHER:	OTHER:	OTHER:	OTHER:

FRIDAY ______	SATURDAY ______	SUNDAY ______	NOTES
APPOINTMENTS/MTGS:	APPOINTMENTS/MTGS:	APPOINTMENTS/MTGS:	

PROJECT PLAN (continued)

SCHEDULE & TIMELINE

As with any product launch, it is important to set deadlines, a timeline and a launch date. As you work on launching your life, it is important to understand where your time is going and to understand your timeline.

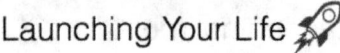

We learned about some process tips at the beginning:

- Write things down
- Get in the zone
- 15-minute sprints
- 80/20 rule
- Law of diminishing returns

You should start the beginning of each week with clear goals as to the top things you want to accomplish. Imagine it's the day before vacation. What are the essentials that have to happen today before you can leave on vacation? It helps you to focus on what is important to reach your goals and what is "busy" work.

These next pages are to help you do a time study for a week.
Track where your time is going. It will help you see where you are spending your time and find ways to be more productive.

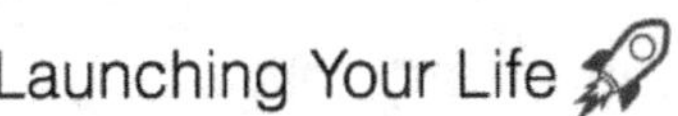

WHERE IS YOUR TIME GOING? – DAILY LOG *EXAMPLE*

TODAY IS MON JUN 6	START	END	TOTAL TIME	WORK LOG	EMAIL	MTG	ACTUAL WORK	OTHER
Get up	6:30			8 - 9 am				
Exercise								
Breakfast	6:45	7:00	15 min	9 - 10 am	45 min			15 min Answer
Other (Lunches/Laundry)	7:00	7:30	30 min					questions abt Proj A
Get ready	7:30	8:30	1 hr.	10 - 11 am			☺ Proj B 1 hr	
Commute to work	8:30	9:00	30 min					
Lunch	12:15	12:25	10 min	11 - 12 pm	30 min		Proj C 15 min	30 min Look for
Commute from work	5:30	6:30	1 hr.					files for Proj A
After Work:				12 - 1 pm			Review notes abt	Lunch 10 min
							Proj B 15 min	Proj A/B ?? 30 min
				1 - 2 pm			Proj A 1 hr	
Dinner	7:15	8:00	45 min	2 - 3 pm	30 min	Talk w/ team 30 min		
After Dinner:								
TV/Computer	8:00	11:00	3 hrs	3 - 4 pm		Talk with boss 30 min	Proj A 15 min	Answer questions
Read								abt Proj B 15 min
Other				4 - 5 pm	15 min		Proj C 15 min	Answer questions
Other							☺ Proj B 15 min	abt Proj C 15 min
Go to Bed				5 - 6 pm	30 min			
				6 - 7 pm				
				7 - 8 pm				
				TOTALS	2 ½ hours	3 hrs	Proj A 15 min	1hr 15 Interruptions/
							Proj B/C 30 min	Questions abt Proj

☺ Mark when it was something you enjoyed/when you were "in the zone," focused and productive.

NOTES

(Observations about how things went today: what went well, what could be improved, what did you accomplish)

Lots of starts and stops. Spent 3 hours in meetings; 2 ½ hours answering emails and 1 hr 15 answering questions about projects. Only worked 15 – 30 minutes on each project. Didn't have any break – 10 min at desk for lunch. Instead of the random interruptions about the projects where I'm answering the same questions - maybe I could send out a short update at the beginning of the week to keep everyone updated. 3 hrs of TV – really?

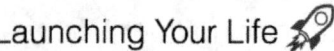

WHERE IS YOUR TIME GOING? – DAILY LOG

TODAY IS	START	END	TOTAL TIME	WORK LOG	EMAIL	MTG	WORK	OTHER
Get up				8 - 9 am				
Exercise								
Breakfast				9 - 10 am				
Other								
Get ready				10 - 11 am				
Commute to work								
Lunch				11 - 12 pm				
Commute from work								
After Work:				12 - 1 pm				
				1 - 2 pm				
Dinner				2 - 3 pm				
After Dinner:								
TV/Computer				3 - 4 pm				
Read								
Other				4 - 5 pm				
Other								
Go to Bed				5 - 6 pm				
				6 - 7 pm				
				7 - 8 pm				
				TOTALS				

☺ Mark when it was something you enjoyed/when you were "in the zone," focused and productive.

NOTES

(Observations about how things went today: what went well, what could be improved, what did you accomplish)

WHERE IS YOUR TIME GOING? – DAILY LOG

TODAY IS	START	END	TOTAL TIME	WORK LOG	EMAIL	MTG	WORK	OTHER
Get up				8 - 9 am				
Exercise								
Breakfast				9 - 10 am				
Other								
Get ready				10 - 11 am				
Commute to work								
Lunch				11 - 12 pm				
Commute from work								
After Work:				12 - 1 pm				
				1 - 2 pm				
Dinner				2 - 3 pm				
After Dinner:								
TV/Computer				3 - 4 pm				
Read								
Other				4 - 5 pm				
Other								
Go to Bed				5 - 6 pm				
				6 - 7 pm				
				7 - 8 pm				
				TOTALS				

☺ Mark when it was something you enjoyed/when you were "in the zone," focused and productive.

NOTES

(Observations about how things went today: what went well, what could be improved, what did you accomplish)

WHERE IS YOUR TIME GOING? – DAILY LOG

TODAY IS	START	END	TOTAL TIME	WORK LOG	EMAIL	MTG	WORK	OTHER
Get up				8 - 9 am				
Exercise								
Breakfast				9 - 10 am				
Other								
Get ready				10 - 11 am				
Commute to work								
Lunch				11 - 12 pm				
Commute from work								
After Work:				12 - 1 pm				
				1 - 2 pm				
Dinner				2 - 3 pm				
After Dinner:								
TV/Computer				3 - 4 pm				
Read								
Other				4 - 5 pm				
Other								
Go to Bed				5 - 6 pm				
				6 - 7 pm				
				7 - 8 pm				
				TOTALS				

☺ Mark when it was something you enjoyed/when you were "in the zone," focused and productive.

NOTES

(Observations about how things went today: what went well, what could be improved, what did you accomplish)

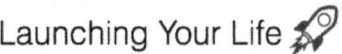

WHERE IS YOUR TIME GOING? – DAILY LOG

TODAY IS	START	END	TOTAL TIME	WORK LOG	EMAIL	MTG	WORK	OTHER
Get up				8 - 9 am				
Exercise								
Breakfast				9 - 10 am				
Other								
Get ready				10 - 11 am				
Commute to work								
Lunch				11 - 12 pm				
Commute from work								
After Work:				12 - 1 pm				
				1 - 2 pm				
Dinner				2 - 3 pm				
After Dinner:								
TV/Computer				3 - 4 pm				
Read								
Other				4 - 5 pm				
Other								
Go to Bed				5 - 6 pm				
				6 - 7 pm				
				7 - 8 pm				
				TOTALS				

☺ Mark when it was something you enjoyed/when you were "in the zone," focused and productive.

NOTES

(Observations about how things went today: what went well, what could be improved, what did you accomplish)

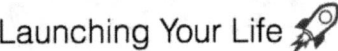

WHERE IS YOUR TIME GOING? – DAILY LOG

TODAY IS	START	END	TOTAL TIME	WORK LOG	EMAIL	MTG	WORK	OTHER
Get up				8 - 9 am				
Exercise								
Breakfast				9 - 10 am				
Other								
Get ready				10 - 11 am				
Commute to work								
Lunch				11 - 12 pm				
Commute from work								
After Work:				12 - 1 pm				
				1 - 2 pm				
Dinner				2 - 3 pm				
After Dinner:								
TV/Computer				3 - 4 pm				
Read								
Other				4 - 5 pm				
Other								
Go to Bed				5 - 6 pm				
				6 - 7 pm				
				7 - 8 pm				
				TOTALS				

☺ Mark when it was something you enjoyed/when you were "in the zone," focused and productive.

NOTES

(Observations about how things went today: what went well, what could be improved, what did you accomplish)

 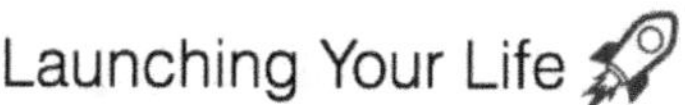

WHERE IS YOUR TIME GOING? – DAILY LOG

TODAY IS	START	END	TOTAL TIME	WORK LOG	EMAIL	MTG	WORK	OTHER
Get up				8 - 9 am				
Exercise								
Breakfast				9 - 10 am				
Other								
Get ready				10 - 11 am				
Commute to work								
Lunch				11 - 12 pm				
Commute from work								
After Work:				12 - 1 pm				
				1 - 2 pm				
Dinner				2 - 3 pm				
After Dinner:								
TV/Computer				3 - 4 pm				
Read								
Other				4 - 5 pm				
Other								
Go to Bed				5 - 6 pm				
				6 - 7 pm				
				7 - 8 pm				
				TOTALS				

☺ Mark when it was something you enjoyed/when you were "in the zone," focused and productive.

NOTES

(Observations about how things went today: what went well, what could be improved, what did you accomplish)

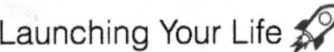

WHERE IS YOUR TIME GOING? – DAILY LOG

TODAY IS	START	END	TOTAL TIME	WORK LOG	EMAIL	MTG	WORK	OTHER
Get up				8 - 9 am				
Exercise								
Breakfast				9 - 10 am				
Other								
Get ready				10 - 11 am				
Commute to work								
Lunch				11 - 12 pm				
Commute from work								
After Work:				12 - 1 pm				
				1 - 2 pm				
Dinner				2 - 3 pm				
After Dinner:								
TV/Computer				3 - 4 pm				
Read								
Other				4 - 5 pm				
Other								
Go to Bed				5 - 6 pm				
				6 - 7 pm				
				7 - 8 pm				
				TOTALS				

☺ Mark when it was something you enjoyed/when you were "in the zone," focused and productive.

NOTES

(Observations about how things went today: what went well, what could be improved, what did you accomplish)

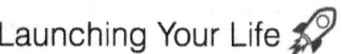

WHERE IS YOUR TIME GOING? – DAILY LOG

TODAY IS	START	END	TOTAL TIME	WORK LOG	EMAIL	MTG	WORK	OTHER
Get up				8 - 9 am				
Exercise								
Breakfast				9 - 10 am				
Other								
Get ready				10 - 11 am				
Commute to work								
Lunch				11 - 12 pm				
Commute from work								
After Work:				12 - 1 pm				
				1 - 2 pm				
Dinner				2 - 3 pm				
After Dinner:								
TV/Computer				3 - 4 pm				
Read								
Other				4 - 5 pm				
Other								
Go to Bed				5 - 6 pm				
				6 - 7 pm				
				7 - 8 pm				
				TOTALS				

☺ Mark when it was something you enjoyed/when you were "in the zone," focused and productive.

NOTES

(Observations about how things went today: what went well, what could be improved, what did you accomplish)

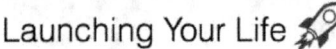

WHERE IS YOUR TIME GOING - SUMMARY

After you complete the daily logs, total up the time spent per week here. Take a look at where your time is going.

ACTION	MON	TUE	WED	THU	FRI	SAT	SUN	TOTAL TIME
Get Ready for work								
Exercising								
Commuting								
At Lunch								
Watching TV								
Social Media								
Reading								
Chores/Tasks								
Email								
Meetings								
Project Work								
Other								

How are you spending your time?

I get up at _________ and leave for work at ___________. That's __________ hours.

I leave work at _________ and go to bed at ___________. That's __________ hours.

I have an hour for lunch every day. What am I doing during that time? What could I do?

What were the things that you enjoyed and were "in the zone"? ☺

Where could you make changes?
Say NO to some things? Find systems to manage your email? Get up a little earlier? Take control of your schedule? Use technology to solve repetitive tasks? What things could you stop doing? What could you give to someone else? Share tasks at home with others? Turn off the TV?

___

___

___

___

___

LAUNCHING YOUR LIFE

10. PURPOSE

As we talked about in the beginning, your purpose is the "sweet spot" in the middle of what you love, what you are great at, what you are paid for and what the world needs. It is a work in progress. You need to take small, continuous action steps to discover what you want and what you need to do to get there.

There is a reason this workbook is only a 90-day plan. Life is always changing, along with your goals and priorities. It is a good idea to take a deep breath and stop and see how you are doing. You can take a fresh look at where you are, what's stopping you and what you need to do to get past the roadblocks.

Einstein said the definition of insanity is doing the same thing over and over again and expecting a different result. If YOU want a different result from what you're doing now, you have to do something different. If your old ways of working, aren't working, it's time to try something else.

For entrepreneurs, we call it **pivot** or **persevere.** They are constantly striving for feedback from their customers to see what they think and how the company is doing. If customers don't like the product or aren't converting on the marketing copy, companies need to *pivot* - or change something. Or, it may be that things *are* working, but times are *tough* and you have to figure out what to do so you can persevere.

Take a breath and ask yourself where you need to *pivot* or what you need to do to *persevere.*

This workbook gave you the fundamentals of taking things one step at a time. Launching something new takes structure and discipline and momentum. You need to start each week with a plan and know what your goals are. You need to assess how things are going and where you are getting results. Talk to your "customers" (your boss, potential employers, colleagues) for feedback and make adjustments.

It is about finding people who can help support you and push you forward. It is about developing your entrepreneurial mindset and embracing challenges to launch a life you love.

Want to keep moving forward?

Sign up for a *Launching Your Life* workshop, and we'll help you get clear on your goals, stay motivated and be accountable.

Check out the programs and workshops at:
www.YearofAction.com
www.LaunchingYour.Life

Contact us at:
LYL@YearofAction.com

NOTES

NOTES

NOTES

NOTES

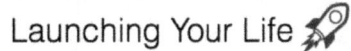

NOTES

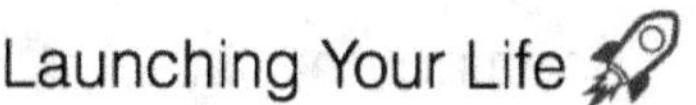

NOTES

NOTES

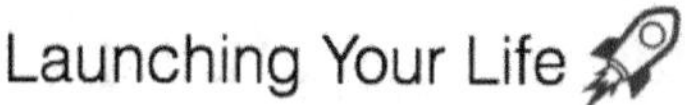

NOTES

NOTES

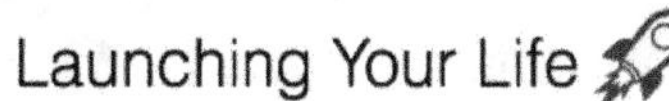

NOTES

NOTES

ABOUT THE AUTHOR

Erin Moran McCormick is an entrepreneur, educator, techie and award-winning designer. She works with executives, entrepreneurs, emerging leaders and students from around the world to develop their entrepreneurial mindset and to teach them how to turn ideas into action.

Erin is the founder of Year of Action and the Director of the Center for Innovation & Entrepreneurship at UMass Boston where her focus is on advancing women.

She has started three companies, been CIO twice and was the former Director of Curriculum Innovation & Technology at Babson College - #1 in the world for entrepreneurship education.

Erin is the author of ***Year of Action – How to Stop Waiting & Start Living Your BIG, Fabulous Life*** - adventures, advice and action steps to create the life you want. The book was a catalyst to create action-based, online business programs for women. It takes the intimidation out of business education and teaches business essentials in a relaxed and inviting environment. It's the combination of the hard and soft skills needed to succeed today. It was written up in *Forbes* saying, "Erin knows what it takes to bring an idea to life. The timing is ripe for a program like this…"

Erin was recently honored as a Distinguished Alumni from Worcester Public Schools and was awarded a key to the city. She earned her degree in art and psychology from Smith College and lives outside of Boston with her husband and two children.

CONTACT INFORMATION:

To contact Erin to speak at your organization or event, email:
Erin@YearofAction.com

Check out the programs and workshops at:
www.YearofAction.com
www.LaunchingYour.Life

www.ingramcontent.com/pod-product-compliance
Lightning Source LLC
Chambersburg PA
CBHW081834170526
45167CB00007B/2798

* 9 7 8 1 5 4 2 8 2 8 5 6 7 *